BARRON'S

Gunther Schmida

Rainbowfish

Photographs: Gunther Schmida
Illustrations: Renate Holzner

CONTENTS

TYPICAL RAINBOWFISH

- Interesting behavior during courtship.

- Two dorsal fins of different lengths.

- Easy to breed.

- Impressive finnage.

- Flashy colors; males usually more colorful than females.

- Most species with gaudily colored courtship stripes.

- Peaceful and gregarious.

- Well suited for community tanks.

- Can change the colors of their scales in a fraction of a second.

Rainbowfish come from all types of aquatic environments in Australia, New Guinea, and a few offshore islands. They are frequently found there, often representing the most important part of the local fish fauna. Although the first species of rainbowfish to be introduced have been kept in aquariums for more than 70 years, these beautiful fish never managed to achieve the popularity of other ornamental fish. As a result of new discoveries during the last 25 years, this attitude has largely changed. Since then, some of the most beautiful rainbowfish have enriched our aquariums.

TO HELP YOU DECIDE

1 Rainbowfish are easy to breed and will even spawn in the community aquarium. However, the young fish (fry) seldom survive in such a situation.

2 Rearing the fry is not too difficult if they are kept in a separate tank.

3 Rainbowfish do not have any special requirements for water hardness or pH. Nevertheless, the water must be changed regularly.

4 Some species are also suitable for keeping at cooler temperatures.

5 Rainbowfish are robust fish that seldom get sick under normal aquarium conditions.

6 Rainbowfish come in various sizes. Thus, there is a fish for every aquarium.

7 Many species can live for six years or more in the aquarium.

8 They eagerly accept flakes or other commercially available food, but should also get live food from time to time.

9 They like to be kept in small schools, but are also happy in communities with other species.

10 They are flexible and do not mind experiments in keeping and care.

In the typical display tanks at the pet store, there is barely a hint of the normal brilliant coloration of rainbowfish. This unfortunate fact has long stood in the way of their popularity. In addition, they grow rather slowly as compared with many other fish, and it takes one to two years before you can enjoy their true beauty in an aquarium. But this waiting period is rewarded in the end. Anyone who has ever seen the splen-

did colors of courting male rainbowfish, regardless of which species, will never forget the show.

To give you some idea of this show, the photos presented in this book are primarily those showing courtship behavior. Despite the best materials and techniques, however, this can only be an indication of the actual process. A photo unfortunately stands still. You must see these fish in action yourself!

SPECIES AND NATURAL HABITAT

When you first see large species like Red, Boeseman's, or Banded Rainbowfish in the pet dealer's display tank or at a fellow aquarist's home, they make a lasting impression. It will probably not be too long before these fish are swimming at your home, too.

How Rainbowfish Were Discovered

When the English scientist John Richardson described the first rainbowfish from a stream near Port Essington on the Cobourg Peninsula, Australia, in 1843, he named it *Atherina nigrans* and assigned it to the silversides.

In 1862, the American ichthyologist Thomas Gill was the first to recognize that this species did not belong to the true silversides, and he placed it in a new genus, Melanotaenia, which means black stripe. It was Gill again who assigned the genus Melanotaenia to its own subfamily—Melanotaeniinae.

Over time, additional species of rainbowfish were discovered and described. However, it was not until 1964 that the Australian scientist Ian Munro gave the rainbowfish the status of a separate family, the Melanotaeniidae.

Dr. Gerald Allen, Curator of Fishes at the Western Australian Museum in Perth, is responsible for ending the long-standing confusion regarding the affiliation of many species and their exact scientific names. In 1974 he had discovered a new species of rainbowfish in tropical Australia, and this aroused his curiosity. Soon he was travelling throughout Australia and New Guinea. New Guinea is still considered largely unexplored even today. It is no wonder, then, that most of the new species of rainbowfish described over the last three decades come from there. The credit for the majority of these newly discovered fish goes to Dr. Allen.

Where Do You Get Rainbowfish?

Most of the known species from New Guinea are available in pet stores in Europe. The situation is somewhat worse for Australian species, because the authorities there have imposed a very extensive ban on commercial exportation of all living things. Therefore, many of these species reach Europe and the United States by airmail in the form of fertilized eggs. For this

*wo displaying Banded Rainbowfish
1. trifasciata) males from Pappan Creek,
ape York Peninsula. 6 in. (15 cm).*

purpose the eggs along with some spawning substrate are placed in small glass containers, so-called vials.

To obtain less common rainbowfish species, I suggest that you become a member of the International Rainbowfish Association (address see page 62). Members of this society are doing their best to obtain new species and distribute them for aquarium hobbyists.

Things to Know before You Buy

Do not be confused if the fish in the pet store are not especially colorful. In most cases, these young fish will develop the coloration typical of the species with time. Furthermore, rainbowfish do not like to live in bare tanks where they are constantly being disturbed.

If you already have an aquarium, then its size will determine which species you will buy. A rule of thumb is that the tank length must be at least ten times the body length of the fully grown fish. In addition, because rainbowfish are schooling fish, they should always be kept in groups of 8–10.

What to Look Out For

Before you decide to buy, it is good to observe the fish in the dealer's aquarium.

Do not buy if

✔ there are any fish in a display tank with signs of a disease, such as white spot, columnaris disease, or fin and tail rot (see page 47);
✔ fish gasp for oxygen at the water surface and breathe rapidly in mid-water;
✔ their gill covers appear to be flared;
✔ the gills at the throat are visible;
✔ the mouth is constantly open, reddened inside, or has cottony growths;
✔ the throat looks reddish;
✔ fish have sores on the body or head;
✔ fins are severely damaged, incomplete, or even absent;
✔ fins are inflamed;
✔ gill covers are partially or entirely absent;
✔ fish are emaciated and have a sunken belly;
✔ the spine is curved, twisted;
✔ worms hang from the throat or out of the vent; or
✔ fish wobble and have a blackish discoloration on half or parts of the body.

After buying, lay the transport bag in the aquarium to let the water temperatures equalize.

Rainbowfish with the above-mentioned signs are usually incurably ill. Although fish with spinal curvatures or missing body parts can survive, under no circumstances should they be used for breeding.

Introducing the Fish

Even if your newly acquired fish look perfect to the naked eye, you should first put them in a quarantine tank at home. In this way you prevent the accidental introduction of disease.

This is how you go about adding the fish:

✔ Lay the transport bag in the aquarium for a short time so that the water temperatures can equalize.

✔ Measure the pH in the bag and in the tank.

✔ Gradually, with long pauses, let the water from the aquarium flow into the bag.

✔ If the pH values are approximately the same, the fish can be released into the tank after about 20–30 minutes.

✔ For greater differences, the acclimation may take longer, and the fish should remain under observation.

✔ Give your new fish more attention than usual for a few days.

TIP

Legal Questions Regarding the Aquarium

Tenancy law: Even if house pets are expressly forbidden in the lease, you may keep ornamental fish in an aquarium. However, you are responsible for ensuring that no damage is done to the dwelling or the building structure because of the aquarium. The landlord may require that you purchase aquarium liability insurance.

Insurance: You can aquire insurance for water damage. Many aquarium organizations offer tank liability or personal indemnity insurance. However, you must be a member of the organization.

Consumer law: If a fish was already sick at the time of purchase, the pet dealer must take it back or reduce the price. For the consumer, it is difficult to establish proof of the fact of disease. The best thing to do is to consult an experienced veterinarian. If you want to exercise your warranty rights, this must be done within 6 months after the purchase.

Children under the age of 16 may not buy fish without the permission of a parent or guardian. If necessary, the dealer must take the animal back and refund the purchase price.

Animal protection: The purchase of the fish obligates you to care for them properly.

Disposing of dead fish: Fish that have died may be buried in the garden. There are no laws regardin the disposal of ornamental fish carcasses.

The Brisbane River with dense stands of ottelia, habitat of the Crimson-spotted Rainbowfish [Large Rainbowfish] (**M. duboulayi**).

Where Do Rainbowfish Live?

Rainbowfish are found in all types of native aquatic environments. There, they are often the most common and most visible representatives of the underwater world.

Most species live in jungle streams or rivers with soft, acidic water often stained brown by humic acids. That does not mean, however, that rainbowfish species must also be provided with such conditions in the aquarium. Rainbowfish are adapted to varying conditions, because even in nature the water conditions can change suddenly after a heavy shower. Experience has also shown that many species do better in an aquarium with hard water and a higher pH.

The Genera of Rainbowfish

The Family Melanotaeniidae is presently divided into six genera with a total of 61 species.
✔ According to genetic studies, the Australian genus *Cairnsichthys* should be more closely allied with the blue eyes (Family Pseudo-mugiliidae); however, in this book it is still assigned to the rainbowfish.
✔ The genus *Chilatherina*, with 10 species, is mainly distributed to the north of the central mountain range in New Guinea. Only one species is also present in a small area to the south.

✔ The genus *Glossolepis* also inhabits the northern part of New Guinea. Like *Chilatherina*, it occurs in all types of waters. Only six species are known so far.

✔ The genus *Iriatherina* contains only one species, the Threadfin Rainbowfish (*Iriatherina werneri*). It is distinguished from all other rainbowfish by its delicate-looking body structure, elongated rays in the second dorsal fin and anal and caudal fins, and by its sail-like first dorsal fin.

✔ Like the genus *Iriatherina*, the numerous species of the genus *Melanotaenia* live in New Guinea and in Australia, where 10 of the 42 species are found. This genus can be divided into five easily distinguishable groups based on differences in appearance.

Tropical savanna waters—habitat of the Western Rainbowfish [Western Splendid Rainbowfish] (M. splendida australis).

✔ So far only the extremely variable species Ornate Rainbowfish (*Rhadinocentrus ornatus*) belongs to the Australian genus *Rhadinocentrus*. It has a very limited distribution on the eastern coast of Australia.

A courtship stripe (see illustration, page 26) is displayed by all members of the genera *Chilatherina*, *Glossolepis*, *Iriatherina*, and *Rhadinocentrus*. It also occurs in most species of the genus *Melanotaenia*.

Aquarium Species

The individual species are arranged alphabetically by genus. The species within the genus *Melanotaenia* are grouped according to their natural relationships.

The English names of most species are those used by Dr. Allen. Some older names are used again; others I have coined in order to better characterize the fish.

The scientific names conform with the most recent status.

Cairns Rainbowfish

Cairnsichthys rhombosomoides (see page 17)
Size: Up to 4 in. (10 cm).
Distribution: In mountain streams between Cardwell and Cairns in northeastern Australia.
Temperature: 18–25°C.
Care: Susceptible to shock, but very persistent after acclimatization. Likes long tanks. Peaceful omnivore, live and frozen food are recommended. Schooling fish.

Axelrod's Rainbowfish

Chilatherina axelrodi
Size: Up to 4.8 in. (12 cm).
Distribution: Only known from forest streams in a small area in northern Papua New Guinea near the border with Irian Jaya.
Temperature: 24–27°C.
Care: Simple; no special requirements of food and water. Schooling fish; needs tank at least 11 yards (3 m) in length; good in a community tank with other peaceful fish.

Bleher's Rainbowfish

Chilatherina bleheri (see pages 17, 53)
Size: Up to 5.5 in. (14 cm).
Distribution: Only known from Danau Bira (Lake Holmes) in the lower Mamberamo River system, Irian Jaya.

Temperature: 25–28°C.
Care: Simple; no special requirements; lively schooling fish that gets along well with other fish, but because of its size needs spacious tanks.
Special note: The males are quite variably colored.

Bulolo Rainbowfish

Chilatherina bulolo (see page 2)
Size: Up to 3.5 in. (9 cm).
Distribution: Lives in the Markham and Ramu river systems in northeastern New Guinea in swift-flowing water.
Temperature: 22–26°C.
Care: Considered to be difficult. Needs long tanks with currents. Lively. Live and frozen food are important. Good in a community tank with equally lively fish.

Highlands Rainbowfish

Chilatherina campsi (see page 16)
Size: Up to 3.5 in. (9 cm).
Distribution: In the upper courses of the Markham, Ramu, Sepik, and Purari Rivers in the highlands of Papua New Guinea.
Temperature: 23–25°C.
Care: Simple; no special requirements; lively schooling fish that does well in a community tank with other species.

Barred Rainbowfish

Chilatherina fasciata (see page 17)
Size: Up to 5.5 in. (14 cm).
Distribution: In the area between the Markham and Mamberamo rivers in northern New Guinea. Inhabits all types of aquatic environments.
Temperature: 26-32°C.
Care: Simple; no special requirements; should only be kept in spacious tanks; peaceful schooling fish.

Red Rainbowfish

Glossolepis incisus (see pages 44, 52, 56)
   Size: Up to 6 in. (15 cm).
   Distribution: Lives in Lake Sentani and its tributary streams near the city of Jayapura in northeastern Irian Jaya.
   Temperature: 22–28°C.
   Care: Simple; because of its size should only be kept in tanks with a capacity of at least 600 L; omnivore; schooling fish; good in a community tank.
   Special notes: If water is kept too warm, only the strongest male displays the magnificent red coloration. The other males are reddish brown. At temperatures around 22°C, males are usually red and the females are silvery with a tinge of yellow.

Spotted Rainbowfish

Glossolepis maculosus (see page 17)
   Size: Up to 2.5 in. (7 cm).
   Distribution: In slow-flowing streams and heavily vegetated ponds in the Markham and Ramu river systems of northern Papua New Guinea.

   Temperature: 25–28°C.
   Care: Easy; likes densely planted aquaria; peaceful omnivore that can be kept in a community tank with other smaller fish.

Sepik Rainbowfish

Glossolepis multisquamatus (see page 1)
   Size: Up to 5.5 in. (14 cm).
   Distribution: In the area of the Ramu and Sepik rivers, especially in swamps, ponds, and lakes of the lowlands.
   Temperature: 26–30°C.
   Care: Simple; should only be kept in large tanks.

Fringefin Rainbowfish

Glossolepis cf. multisquamatus (see page 17)
   Size: Up to 4.8 in. (12 cm).
   Distribution: So far known only from Lake Kli in the Mamberamo River system in northern Irian Jaya.
   Temperature: 25–28°C.
   Care: Simple; peaceful schooling fish without special requirements.

Lake Wanam Rainbowfish

Glossolepis wanamensis (see page 9)
   Size: Up to 6 in. (15 cm).
   Distribution: Known only from Lake Wanam near the town of Lae, northeastern New Guinea.
   Temperature: 28–30°C.
   Care: Simple; placid, undemanding schooling fish for larger well-planted tanks; omnivore.
   Special notes: The species *Glossolepis wanamensis*, *G. cf. multisquamatus*, and *G. multisquamatus* seem to be closely related.

The Lake Wanam Rainbowfish can grow to 6 in. (15 cm) in length.

PORTRAITS I:
RAINBOWFISH

Rainbowfish are found in Australia and New Guinea in 6 genera with 61 species. Because new species are still being found, this number will surely increase in the future.

Photo above: Elongated fins distinguish the Threadfin Rainbowfish from its relatives. 2 in. (5 cm).

Photo above: The male Highlands Rainbowfish in full colors. 2.5 in. (7 cm).

Photo right: The Lake Tebera Rainbowfish is among the most magnificent species. 3 in. (8 cm).

Photo left: Male Fringefin Rainbowfish from Lake Kli. 4 in. (10 cm).

Photo right: The coloration of Bleher's Rainbowfish males can vary in intensity. 4 in. (10 cm).

Photo above: Cairns Rainbowfish inhabits swift-flowing mountain streams. 3 in. (8 cm).

Photo left: The Barred Rainbowfish is widely distributed in northern New Guinea. 4 in. (10 cm).

Photo below: The Spotted Rainbowfish grows to only 2 in. (6 cm) in length.

Ramu Rainbowfish

Glossolepis ramuensis
   Size: Up to 3 in. (8 cm).
   Distribution: In forest streams in the Ramu
and Gogol river valley in northern Papua New
Guinea.
   Temperature: 25–28°C.
   Care: Simple; as an active swimmer, it should
be kept in larger tanks; peaceful omnivore.

Threadfin Rainbowfish

Iriatherina werneri (see pages 16, 19)
   Size: Up to 2 in. (5 cm).
   Distribution: In weed-choked ponds, cut-off
arms of rivers, and swamps in the southern
lowlands of New Guinea, in the northern half
of the Cape York Peninsula, and in scattered
localities in Arnhem Land in northern Australia.
   Temperature: 25–30°C.
   Care: Simple; best kept alone or with small
fish; peaceful omnivore; schooling fish; likes
densely planted tanks.

Northern Rainbowfish

Melanotaenia affinis (see page 25)
   Size: 5.5 in. (14 cm).
   Distribution: In all types of aquatic habitats
from the Markham to the Mamberamo river
system in northern New Guinea.
   Temperature: 24–28°C.
   Care: Easy; undemanding species; needs large
tanks.

Arfak Rainbowfish

Melanotaenia arfakensis (see page 53)
   Size: Up to 4 in. (10 cm).
   Distribution: In waters of the Prafi Plains in
the northeastern Vogelkop Peninsula, Irian Jaya.
   Temperature: 24–28°C.
   Care: Simple; undemanding omnivore; needs
medium-size tank.

Boeseman's Rainbowfish

Melanotaenia boesemani (see back cover)
   Size: Up to 5.5 in. (14 cm).
   Distribution: Only in Lakes Ayamaru, Hain
and Aitinjo and their tributaries in the center
of the Vogelkop Peninsula, Irian Jaya.
   Temperature: 25–28°C.
   Care: Simple; should not be kept in tanks
with a capacity of less than 157 gallons
(600 L); omnivore; very lively schooling fish.

Sorong Rainbowfish

Melanotaenia fredericki
   Size: Up to 4.5 in. (12 cm).
   Distribution: In small streams near the
town of Sorong in the northwestern Vogelkop
Peninsula, Irian Jaya.
   Temperature: 25–28°C.
   Care: Simple; needs large tanks; peaceful
omnivore.

Goldie River Rainbowfish

Melanotaenia goldiei (see page 25)
   Size: Up to 5.5 in. (14 cm).
   Distribution: In all types of aquatic habitats
in southern New Guinea.
   Temperature: 18–27°C.
   Care: Simple; needs large tanks; omnivore;
peaceful schooling fish.

Lake Tebera Rainbowfish

Melanotaenia herbertaxelrodi (see page 16)
   Size: Up to 5.5 in. (14 cm).
   Distribution: Only in Lake Tebera and its
tributaries in the Southern Highlands of
Papua New Guinea.
   Temperature: 21–24°C.
   Care: Simple; undemanding schooling fish;
should be kept in tank with a capacity of at
least 157 gallons (600 L); lively omnivore; needs
enough open space to swim.

Lake Kutubu Rainbowfish
Melanotaenia lacustris (see pages 21, 32, 37)
Size: Up to 4.5 in. (12 cm).
Distribution: Only in Lake Kutubu and its outlet in the Southern Highlands of Papua New Guinea.
Temperature: 20–25°C.
Care: Simple; undemanding; very peaceful schooling fish; omnivore.

Lakamora Rainbowfish
Melanotaenia lakamora (see page 21)
Size: Up to 2.5 in. (7 cm).
Distribution: In Lakes Lakamora and Aiwaso in southwestern Irian Jaya.
Temperature: 24–28°C.
Care: Simple; peaceful schooling fish; can be kept in smaller tanks; omnivore.

Special notes: This species was first discovered in 1995 in the Triton Lakes region, southwestern Irian Jaya.

Batanta Island Rainbowfish
Melanotaenia cf. misoolensis (see page 20)
Size: Up to 4 in. (10 cm).
Distribution: Forest streams on Batanta Island, west of the Vogelkop Peninsula, Irian Jaya.
Temperature: 22–28°C.
Care: Simple; undemanding; peaceful schooling fish; omnivore.

Mountain Rainbowfish
Melanotaenia monticola (see page 20)
Size: Up to 4.5 in. (12 cm).
Distribution: In mountain streams in the upper Purari and Kikori river systems in the Southern Highlands of Papua New Guinea.
Temperature: 17–23°C.
Care: Easily kept species; tolerates cooler temperatures; peaceful; undemanding.

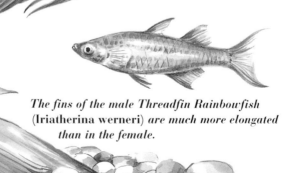

*The fins of the male Threadfin Rainbowfish (**Iriatherina werneri**) are much more elongated than in the female.*

PORTRAITS II:
RAINBOWFISH

In their native Australia and New Guinea, rainbowfish are found in all types of aquatic environments, including streams, rivers, ponds and lakes from the lowlands to the higher elevations.

Photo above: The Batanta Island Rainbowfish is a peaceful schooling fish. 2.5 in. (7 cm).

Photo above: The Mountain Rainbowfish comes from jungle streams of the Southern Highlands in Papua New Guinea. 3 in. (8 cm).

Photo left: The Fly River Rainbowfish is also suitable for smaller aquaria. 2 in. (6 cm).

Photo right: The Dwarf Neon Rainbowfish [Neon Rainbowfish] is one of the most exciting recent finds. 2 in. (6 cm).

Photo right: The Lakamora Rainbowfish was first discovered in 1995 in the Triton Lakes region of southwestern Irian Jaya. 2 in. (5 cm).

Photo below: The Elongated Swordplant is native to northern and northeastern Australia.

Photo above and right: The Lake Kutubu Rainbowfish can change its coloration very quickly from black to black and silver, blue and silver, turquoise and ?, and finally to gold.

Dwarf Neon Rainbowfish [Neon Rainbowfish]

Melanotaenia praecox (see page 20)

Size: Up to 2 in. (6 cm).

Distribution: In small swift-flowing jungle streams in the middle sections of the Mamberamo River system in northern Irian Jaya.

Temperature: 24–27°C.

Care: Undemanding; should be kept in darker tanks because the coloring is seen to best advantage there; peaceful schooling fish; omnivore.

Special notes: Although described back in 1910, this species was first introduced in 1992.

Fly River Rainbowfish

Melanotaenia sexlineata (see page 20)

Size: Up to 2.5 in. (7 cm).

Distribution: So far only from streams in the upper part of the Fly River near the town of Kiunga in western Papua New Guinea.

Temperature: 22–25°C.

Care: Undemanding; peaceful schooling fish; suitable even for small tanks.

Banded Rainbowfish

Melanotaenia trifasciata (see front cover—small picture, pages 8, 24, 25, 36, 61)

Size: Depending on locality, 4–6 in. (10–15 cm).

Distribution: Northern Australia.

Temperature: 24–28°C.

Care: Undemanding; peaceful; suitable for community tanks with other less showy ornamental fish; keep in moderately hard water, although most forms of this species come from soft, slightly acidic waters with no vegetation.

Special notes: So far there are 26 color varieties of 3 different types, distinguishable by body shape.

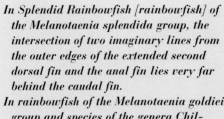

In Splendid Rainbowfish [rainbowfish] of the Melanotaenia splendida group, the intersection of two imaginary lines from the outer edges of the extended second dorsal fin and the anal fin lies very far behind the caudal fin.

In rainbowfish of the Melanotaenia goldiei group and species of the genera Chilatherina and Glossolepis, the intersection of two imaginary lines from the outer edges of the extended second dorsal fin and anal fin lies in the caudal fin or in the caudal peduncle.

In McCulloch's Rainbowfish [Dwarf Rainbowfish] (Melanotaenia maccullochi), the finnage resembles that of the goldiei group. However, in both sexes, the posterior edge of the fin is rounded, and the females are larger than the males.

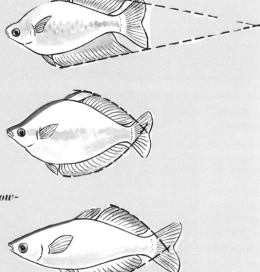

✔ Type 1: Up to 4.5 in. (12 cm) long. Males develop a very deep body shape with increasing age. Occurrence: Northern Territory between the Mary River eastward to the northern region of the Gulf of Carpentaria; Melville Island, north of Darwin.

✔ Type 2: At least 6 in. (15 cm) long. Males can be very deep bodied. Occurrence: In waters west of the divide on the Cape York Peninsula.

✔ Type 3: Males with slender body shape. Occurrence: In waters east of the divide on the Cape York Peninsula.

Exquisite Rainbowfish

Melanotaenia exquisita (see page 24)
Size: Up to 2.5 in. (7 cm).
Distribution: Upper reaches of the South Alligator, Daly, and Mary river systems, Northern Territory, and in the King George River in northwestern Australia.
Temperature: 22–27°C.
Care: Simple; need well-planted tanks; peaceful; undemanding schooling fish.

Waterfall Creek Rainbowfish

Melanotaenia cf. exquisita (see page 24)
Size: Up to 2.5 in. (7 cm).
Distribution: So far known only from the upper Waterfall Creek and South Alligator River, Northern Territory, Australia.
Temperature: 22–25°C.
Care: Like the Exquisite Rainbowfish.
Special notes: Very similar to the Exquisite Rainbowfish. The males of the two species differ, however, in body shape and breeding coloration.

Slender Rainbowfish

Melanotaenia gracilis (see page 25)
Size: Up to 3 in. (8 cm).

Distribution: Drysdale and King Edward river systems in the Kimberley region of northwestern Australia.
Temperature: 23–30°C.
Care: Like the Exquisite Rainbowfish.

Pygmy Rainbowfish [Whitefin Rainbowfish]

Melanotaenia pygmaea
Size: Up to 2 in. (6 cm).
Distribution: Known only from two streams in the Prince Regent River system in the Kimberley region in northwestern Australia.
Temperature: 24–28°C.
Care: Like the Exquisite Rainbowfish.
Special notes: The discovery of this species led to many new discoveries over the last three decades.

Black-banded Rainbowfish

Melanotaenia nigrans (see pages 24, 26)
Size: Up to 3.5 in. (9 cm).
Distribution: Found in four widely separated areas: eastern Kimberley region of Western Australia, northern part of the Northern Territory, Groote Eylandt in the Gulf of Carpentaria, and the tip of the Cape York Peninsula.
Temperature: 22–30°C.
Care: Like the Exquisite Rainbowfish.

Papuan Rainbowfish

Melanotaenia papuae
Size: Up to 3 in. (8 cm).
Distribution: Waters in the area around Port Moresby, Papua New Guinea.
Temperature: 25–30°C.
Care: Like other representatives of this group.
Special notes: Was initially placed in the same species as the Fly River Rainbowfish (*Melanotaenia sexlineata*).

PORTRAITS III: RAINBOWFISH

With good water quality in the aquarium, rainbowfish always appear in their best dress. Water changes stimulate the fish to courtship and spawning.

Photo above: The Waterfall Creek Rainbowfish is so far found only in the Kakadu National Park. 2.5 in. (6.5 cm).

Photo above: The Exquisite Rainbowfish is an undemanding schooling fish. 2 in. (5 cm).

Photo above: Two male Black-banded Rainbowfish present their erected fins. 2.5 in. (6.5 cm).

Photo left: Slender type of the Banded Rainbowfish from the Claudie River. This species also occurs in two deep-bodied types. 4.5 in. (10 cm).

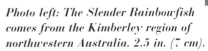

Photo left: The Slender Rainbowfish comes from the Kimberley region of northwestern Australia. 2.5 in. (7 cm).

Photo above: A male Northern Rainbowfish. 4 in. (10 cm).

Photo left: A pair of Goldie River Rainbowfish from Port Moresby, Papua New Guinea. 4 in. (10 cm).

Photo right: Portrait of the Banded Rainbowfish from Running Creek, Cape York Peninsula.

Photo right: The very brittle ottelia is only suitable for larger tanks.

TIP

Separate Tanks

All subspecies of the Splendid Rainbowfish (*Melanotaenia splendida*) must be kept in separate tanks to prevent interbreeding of races. Therefore, be sure to purchase fish only from dealers and breeders who are very knowledgeable and understand their subject.

McCulloch's Rainbowfish [Dwarf Rainbowfish]

Melanotaenia maccullochi (see page 28)
   Size: Depending on origin, 1–2.5 in. (3–7 cm).
   Distribution: Northern Australia, Papua New Guinea.
   Temperature: 22–30°C.
   Care: Simple; undemanding schooling fish; planted tanks and grouping with other fish is suitable. This smallest form from the Northern Territory, which grows to only 1 in. (3 cm), is also content with small tanks.
   Special notes: There are forms which differ in appearance in four widely separated regions. The question of whether we are really dealing with only one species remains to be seen.
   ✔ Region 1: Small streams and swamps in the drainage area of the Fly and Bensbach rivers in southwestern Papua New Guinea.
   ✔ Region 2: Small streams and swamps near the tip of the Cape York Peninsula.
   ✔ Region 3: Jungle streams and swamps in the coastal lowlands between Cardwell and Cooktown on the northeastern coast of Australia (typical form, photo see page 28).

✔ Region 4: Two streams arising in swamps in the vicinity of Litchfield National Park, southwest of Darwin, Northern Territory (smallest form).

Lake Eacham Rainbowfish

Melanotaenia eachamensis
   Size: Up to 3 in. (8 cm).
   Distribution: Originally known only from Lake Eacham, a crater lake in the Atherton Tableland in northeastern Australia; the species has since become extinct there. However, it has been found in other nearby crater lakes and streams.
   Temperature: 20–26°C.
   Care: Simple; undemanding schooling fish; suitable for smaller tanks.

Crimson-spotted Rainbowfish [Large Rainbowfish]

Melanotaenia duboulayi (see pages 4, 27, 48)
   Size: Depending on origin, up to 5 in. (13 cm).
   Distribution: In all types of aquatic environments on Australia's eastern coast from northern Port Macquarie (New South Wales) to north of Bundaberg (Queensland).
   Temperature: 18–28°C.
   Care: Simple; undemanding; needs medium-size tanks; peaceful schooling fish.
   Special notes: The first rainbowfish species to be introduced. For years, the species was believed to be the Black-banded Rainbowfish *(Melanotaenia nigrans)*.

Murray River Rainbowfish
[Inland Rainbowfish]
Melanotaenia fluviatilis
Size: Up to 4 in. (10 cm).
Distribution: Scattered localities in the low-
lands of the Murray-Darling river basin and in
the upper tributaries of the Fitzroy River Basin
in central Queensland, Australia.
Temperature: 15–30°C.
Care: Like the Crimson-spotted Rainbowfish
[Large Rainbowfish]

Splendid Rainbowfish
Melanotaenia splendida
There are five subspecies of this species, four
of which become very large. Their impressive
finnage makes them appear even larger.
Temperature: 24–30°C.
Care: Simple; undemanding; require tanks
with a capacity of at least 157 gallons (600 L);
like rich plant growth.

Western Rainbowfish
[Western Splendid
Rainbowfish]
*Melanotaenia splendida
australis* (see page 41)

Size: Depending on origin, up to 4.5 in. (12 cm).
Distribution: In many color varieties from the
Pilbara region, Western Australia, across the
Kimberley region, northwestern Australia, to
the northern part of the Northern Territory.
Special notes: Some forms of this subspecies
are supposed to be more closely related to
Melanotaenia duboulayi, M. eachamensis, and
M. fluviatilis than to *M. splendida.*

Checkered Rainbowfish
[Checkered Splendid Rainbowfish]
Melanotaenia splendida inornata (see front
cover—large picture, pages 29, 33)
Size: Up to 6 in. (15 cm).
Distribution: In all types of aquatic environments from the Cape York Peninsula west to
the area around Darwin, Northern Territory,
Australia.
Special notes: This form and the subspecies
Red-striped Rainbowfish [Red-striped Splendid
Rainbowfish] (*Melanotaenia splendida rubrostriata*) have the largest second dorsal fin and
anal fin of this species. Older males also
develop an especially striking deep-
bodied shape.

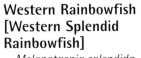

*In most rainbowfish species,
males attract the females with
a courtship stripe (left: Black-
banded Rainbowfish,* Melanotaenia
nigrans*). Only a few species of the
genus* Melanotaenia *do not display
courtship stripes (right: Crimson-
spotted Rainbowfish [Large Rainbow-
fish],* Melanotaenia duboulayi*).*

Red-striped Rainbowfish
[Red-striped Splendid Rainbowfish]
Melanotaenia splendida rubrostriata
    Size: Up to 6 in. (15 cm).
    Distribution: In all types of aquatic environments in southern New Guinea from Etna Bay in Irian Jaya eastward to the Aramia River, Papua New Guinea, as well as the Aru Islands.
    Special notes: During courtship, broad red stripes cover the entire body.

Eastern Rainbowfish
[Eastern Splendid Rainbowfish]
Melanotaenia splendida splendida (see pages 6, 53, 64)
    Size: Up to 6 in. (15 cm).
    Distribution: In all types of aquatic environments on the eastern coast of Australia from

Typical form of McCulloch's Rainbowfish [Dwarf Rainbowfish] (M. macullochi). *It comes from the area around Cairns in northeastern Australia. 2 in. (5 cm).*

the Daintree River in the north to somewhat south of the town of Gladstone.
    Special notes: Many forms of this species need closer investigation.

Desert Rainbowfish
[Desert Splendid Rainbowfish]
Melanotaenia splendida tatei
    Size: Up to 6 in. (15 cm).
    Distribution: In permanent bodies of water of the Lake Eyre Basin in central Australia.

Special notes: Its appearance is like the Checkered Rainbowfish [Checkered Splendid Rainbowfish] (*Melanotaenia splendida inornata*), but is more slender.

Parkinson's Rainbowfish
Melanotaenia parkinsoni (see page 49)
Size: Up to 6 in. (15 cm).
Distribution: In waters between Port Moresby and Milne Bay in southeastern Papua New Guinea.
Temperature: 25–30°C.
Care: Very large species; needs a spacious tank; otherwise no special requirements.
Special notes: Its appearance is most similar to the Eastern Rainbowfish [Eastern Splendid Rainbowfish] (*Melanotaenia splendida splendida*), and it is a close relative of the "splendida" group.

A male Checkered Rainbowfish [Checkered Splendid Rainbowfish] (M. s. inornata) from Anniversary Creek, Northern Territory. 4 in. (10 cm).

Ornate Rainbowfish
Rhadinocentrus ornatus (see pages 51, 53)
Size: Up to 2.5 in. (7 cm).
Distribution: Found along the eastern coast of Australia from north of the town of Coff's Harbour in northern New South Wales to northeast of Rockhampton in central Queensland. Lives mainly in very soft, acidic waters with fine white sandy bottom. Such waters are often tea colored and never very far from the coast.
Temperature: 18–28°C.

Care: Delicate species; regular water changes are important; be careful when moving the fish (see page 37); for advanced hobbyists.

Special notes: A very attractive species of extremely variable coloration. Up to four different color varieties can occur side by side in the same body of water. Entirely red specimens are very rare.

The Community Tank

You can readily keep almost all rainbowfish in a community tank along with peaceful representatives of other fish families. Large robust species even get along with cichlids, provided the latter are not too rough. Even nocturnal fish like catfish do not disturb the rainbowfish, which usually sleep near the surface.

The type of fish you put in your aquarium with your rainbowfish depends on your preferences.

Tip: Only group together fish that have the same water quality, planting, or temperature requirements, and the same temperament and size. Several rainbowfish species can be kept together easily. However, the females of many species as well as many color varieties are very much alike and cannot be differentiated readily. For the aquarist who does not want to breed, this is unimportant. However, a breeder should avoid getting the females mixed up in order to maintain the species and subspecies purely. In nature, hybridization between species living side by side is unknown. However, in the aquarium, it can happen.

A community tank with (from left to right): Red Rainbowfish, Leopard Catfish, Variable Platies, Boeseman's Rainbowfish, Neon Tetras, and Kribensis. (The relative sizes are not to scale.)

These Species Go Together

✔ For rainbowfish up to 2 in. (5 cm) in length, suitable fish are small characins and barbs, catfish, tooth-carps.

✔ For rainbowfish up to 4 in. (10 cm) in length, suitable fish are medium-size characins, barbs, catfish, dwarf cichlids, gouramies, gudgeons and gobies, swordtails.

✔ For rainbowfish more than 4 in. (10 cm) in length, suitable fish are large barbs, characins, cichlids that are not too rough, catfish.

✔ Threadfin Rainbowfish are best kept alone because of the danger that other fish will nibble at their fins. Suitable tank mates are blue-eyes like *Pseudomugil gertrudae.*

The Geo-Tank

It would be ideal to create a community aquarium using only rainbowfish.

Unfortunately, only a few suitable species from this region are available commercially.

Well suited for a community tank with medium-size and large rainbowfish are:

✔ Sleeper gobies of the genus *Hypseleotris.* They will eat any leftover food on the tank bottom.

✔ Smaller representatives of the genera *Oxyeleotris* and *Mogurnda.*

✔ Some species of grunters, Terapontidae.

✔ The peaceful eel-tailed catfish (Plotosiidae) of the genera *Neosilurus* and *Porocheilus.*

✔ Juveniles of all sea catfish (Ariidae).

ROUTINE AQUARIUM MAINTENANCE

An aquarium brings a bit of nature into your home. The fish and plants live under your care, and for them to be comfortable, there are certain requirements of the aquarium habitat that must be met.

Things to Keep in Mind

You have decided on one or several species of rainbowfish. Before buying them and adding them to your tank, however, the aquarium should already be set up (see page 34) and given a 2-week trial run with all the equipment operating (see page 35).

✔ The size of the tank depends on the size of the fish.

✔ Indeed, the biggest mistake all aquarists make in the beginning is overstocking the tank with fish. Therefore, self-control when buying fish is important; otherwise you will have many fish losses. Plus, a tank with fewer fish is easier to maintain.

The Right Location

✔ Rainbowfish do not like to be constantly disturbed or even startled. Therefore, your aquarium should be in a quiet, out-of-the-way spot in the room.

A male Lake Kutubu Rainbowfish (M. lacustris). Body length 3.1 in. (8 cm).

✔ The tank should get only about 1–2 hours of sunlight in the morning. Even the best artificial lighting will never bring out the colors of rainbowfish as well as sunlight can. Use this time to enjoy the brilliant color of your fish.

✔ A tank with 157 gallons (600 L) or more is very heavy. Therefore, the load-bearing capacity of the floor should be tested by an expert before you purchase a tank of this size.

Caution with Electricity

Electrical devices in contact with water must be handled with care. Devices that are used in water must have a notation such as the valid VDE [Association of German Electrical Engineers] or TÜV [Technical Control Board] symbol [Underwriters Laboratories' UL listing mark] stating that they are suitable for use in water. Install a GFCI (ground-fault circuit interrupter) between the devices and the outlet to prevent accidents as much as possible. In any case, always unplug the aquarium before working on it.

This Is What You Need

✔ A sealed all-glass aquarium of the right size with a sturdy base.

✔ An automatic aquarium water heater, a filter, and a thermometer.

✔ A light fixture with fluorescent bulbs which fits on the aquarium.

✔ Fifty-five to sixty-five pounds (25–30 kg) of dark gravel in assorted particle sizes from ⅛–¾ of an in. (2–20 mm)—best mixed from various types.

✔ About a dozen rounded and flattened rocks (pebbles) approximately 4–6 in. (10–15 cm) in length.

✔ A large piece of bogwood (pet store).

✔ A background. Different types are sold in pet stores, either as a printed scene of an aquarium landscape which can be cut to size and attached to the back of the tank or as a molded plastic wall that can be mounted inside the aquarium.

The Tank Size

The size of the aquarium must be appropriate for these active swimmers.

✔ For species less than 2.4 in. (6 cm) in length, a tank measuring 24 × 16 × 16 in. (60 × 40 × 40 cm) (length × width × height) is sufficient.

✔ Species up to 4.5 in. (12 cm) long should be kept in an aquarium with measurements of 25 × 20 × 20 in. (100 × 50 × 50 cm).

✔ Large species up to 6 in. (15 cm) in length need tanks with minimum dimensions of 60 × 24 × 24 in. (150 × 60 × 60 cm). They look even better, though, in more spacious aquaria. However, these giant

The substrate should slope up towards the back.

tanks and the requisite equipment are also more expensive.

Setting up the Aquarium

How you set up the aquarium depends primarily on the species of fish, their size when they are fully grown, and their temperament. Plants cannot be used with many of the species that come from waters which have little or no vegetation. However, most species are so robust that you do not have to be guided by their natural environment in caring for them.

This is how you proceed:

1. After buying the tank, test its watertightness outdoors on a sturdy, level base.

2. Thoroughly wash the gravel which will serve as the substrate and put it into the aquarium. At the

Bogwood

This decoration gives the fish a place to hide. Depending on the appearance of the root, it is placed at an angle from a back corner diagonally toward the front or crosswise in the aquarium. At least 1 week before setting up the tank, put the bogwood in water so that it can become saturated.

Adding the Plants

A well-planted tank can be a true feast for the eyes. Begin adding the plants before the aquarium has been completely filled with water.

1. Poke a depression in the gravel with your fingers for each rosette-forming plant.

2. Trim the roots of plants that already have them to about 1.5 in. (4 cm) with scissors. Insert the plants as straight as possible so that the crown remains free.

3. Carefully fill in the hole with gravel, but do not press it down.

Prune bunch plants with scissors and set them in the substrate at an angle. The end is weighted down with a small rock. The right plants for rainbowfish are listed on page 41.

front of the aquarium, it should cover the bottom to a depth of at least 1.2 in. (3 cm). To the back and sides, it is piled up to a depth of about 3.8 in. (10 cm), because it should provide support for the plant roots there.

3. The rocks are scattered at random on the gravel. In the center front, however, there should be an open area.

4. The bogwood is put in place.

5. The tank is now filled about halfway with water from a hose (see page 39).

6. Now the plants are put in.

7. Next, fill the aquarium completely with water, and install the heater and filter where they will be as unobtrusive as possible. The thermometer is attached diagonally across from the heater (see page 39).

8. An aquarium cover prevents excessive evaporation of the heated water and also keeps the fish from jumping out of the tank.

9. Install the lighting.

10. Now switch on all of the devices. The aquarium will be "broken in" during the next 2 weeks. You should give the bacteria and the newly added plants this time to transform the tap water into a medium which is tolerable for fish. For an aquarist, especially a novice, this is the most difficult period. But it is worth the wait!

Lighting

The right lighting is important for plant growth. For this purpose, use 15-watt fluorescent tubes, color temperature 41 [= 2700°K]. Mount the light fixture over the aquarium as far to the front as possible. By doing this, the fish will be illuminated at an angle from the front, and their colors will shine nicely. If the lamps are too far back in the light fixture, the fish are practically seen in backlighting.

Water

There would be no life on Earth without water. In fact, humans are about 60 percent water. Life began in the water, and by far most vertebrates, to say nothing of invertebrates, still live in an aqueous environment. Fish represent the vertebrate group with the most species. In nature, water is not always in an ideal state; however, as a fishkeeper, you have an obligation to adjust the water conditions to meet the requirements of your fish.

Although the rainbowfish family is very adaptable and the water quality in their native waters is often subject to incredible variations, you should try to keep the water conditions in the aquarium constant. Therefore, it is important to know which factors contribute to the health and happiness of your pets.

Water Hardness

Total or general water hardness is measured in parts per million (ppm) of calcium carbonate in the water. Test kits are commercially available for this purpose. As a rule, water with values of 17°dH and above less than 75 ppm is very soft, between 75 and 150 ppm is soft, between 150 and 220 is medium, between 220 and 360 is hard, and anything over 360 ppm is considered very hard.

In their native habitat, rainbowfish live in extremely soft and hard water. I have already measured a water hardness of more than 40°dH in water inhabited by rainbowfish. The fish there looked just as healthy as those from water with no measurable hardness.

Many species from extremely hard water environments are better kept in medium-hard and hard water. For these reasons, water hardness plays only a minor role in maintenance.

The pH Value

The pH value reflects the levels of acids or bases in the water.

pH = 7: neutral.
pH < 7: acidic.
pH > 7: alkaline.

The pH value is defined logarithmically. This means that water with a pH of 6 contains 10 times more acid than water with a pH of 7, and water with a pH of 8 is 10 times more alkaline than neutral water. The value can be determined using test strips, indicator solutions, or even electronically. Ask your pet dealer for advice.

The pH of a body of water can also fluctuate in nature over the course of the day, especially in heavily vegetated waters. Tap water usually has a neutral pH. It is advisable to keep the pH in your aquarium between 6.5 and 7.5. You can best achieve this through regular water changes. Replace

Displaying male Banded Rainbowfish (M. trifasciata). Body length 5.8 in. (15 cm).

one third of the aquarium contents with aged
fresh water, which should have a neutral pH.

Be Careful When Moving

Rainbow fish tolerate fluctuations in pH without problems if this change happens slowly. If
you have several tanks and want to move fish,
do it carefully because too great a difference in
pH and too quick a move can be fatal.

In any case, first test the pH in the respective
aquaria. If you detect differences, proceed as
follows:

1. Put the fish in a large bucket with water
from your tank. Cover the bucket—the fish
jump!

2. Slowly add water from the new tank.

*Rainbowfish—here Lake Kutubu
Rainbowfish* (**Melanotaenia lacustris**)—
are schooling fish.

3. Put the fish in their new home.

Plants in the Aquarium

Few rainbowfish species live in waters where
higher aquatic plants grow. For this reason,
they are also happy in unplanted aquaria that
are only decorated with rocks and roots. Higher
plants in the underwater landscape serve primarily to offer the viewer a pleasant scene and
to bring another aspect of nature into the
home.

Filtration

An aquarium is a tank of water filled with life, with fish, plants, and possibly snails to clean up leftover food and algae. Fish must eat to thrive. They then eliminate all indigestible substances. These remain in the aquarium along with other organic waste products. Over time, through processes of decay, these waste products form substances which are more or less toxic for fish. In addition, a good deal of oxygen is consumed in the process.

To maintain the water quality so that fish can live in it, you must filter the water. External, internal, or undergravel filters are commercially available for this purpose. Ask your pet dealer for advice. The filters are filled with materials such as filter foam, nylon floss, ceramic chips, or activated carbon.

✔ Mechanical filtration: Driven by a pump, the water flows through the filter. In the process, suspended particulates are trapped in the fine-pored filter media.

✔ Biological filtration: This filtration method functions with the aid of bacteria which live in the substrate, in the filter, and in the water. They ingest the waste products from fish digestive processes, uneaten food, or decaying plant matter and break them down into nitrate. Nitrate is toxic and therefore must be occasionally removed through water changes.

✔ The filters must be cleaned occasionally—at the very latest when the water is only flowing through slowly.

Changing the Water

Although filter technology has made enormous progress recently and modern filters, because of the microorganisms colonizing them, can maintain water quality within tolerable limits longer than they used to, you should still change the water occasionally. When and how often you do this depends mainly on the fish population. Fewer fish in the tank and careful feeding mean fewer water changes. But you can never get by entirely without it!

Installing the External Filter

An external filter is located outside the tank and can be used for large or small aquariums. When installing it, make sure the spray bar is just below the surface of the water and that the jets point to the front. The resulting movement of the surface allows the water to absorb more oxygen.

When adding the water, let it flow over a plate.

Pay attention to the following:

✔ The water intended for changes must be aged.

✔ Never replace more than one third of the aquarium contents.

✔ Adjust the temperature and pH value to that of the tank.

✔ Siphon up the excess mulm from the bottom with an aquarium vacuum.

✔ Direct the water flowing from the hose over a plate placed in the aquarium, for example, so that the gravel is not stirred up too much.

Water Temperature

The temperature of the water plays a very important role for the welfare of the fish. As cold-blooded inhabitants of temperate and tropical zones, rainbowfish can only survive within a certain temperature range. Some species can even tolerate summer temperatures outdoors in central Europe [in northern latitudes]. Most species, however, need heated water.

Heating an aquarium does not pose much of a problem today. Pet stores offer many heating devices. The simplest are the automatic aquarium water heaters, because the temperature can be easily regulated with a thermostat. All you have to do is preselect the desired temperature; the thermostat takes care of the rest.

An aerator constantly keeps the water in motion and thus provides a uniform water temperature in the aquarium. In nature, considerable variations in temperature occur in different areas of a body of water, especially a standing one. In nature, however, the fish can choose the area with their preferred temperature. This is not possible in an aquarium.

Important: When changing the water, always make sure that the temperature of the fresh water is the same as that of the aquarium or differs by 1–2°C at most.

Test the temperature of the water daily, especially in the winter, so that you can intervene if the heater fails.

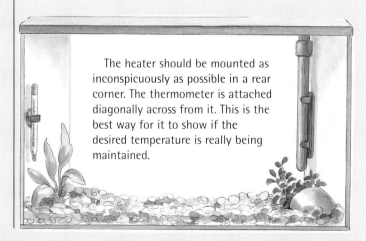

The heater should be mounted as inconspicuously as possible in a rear corner. The thermometer is attached diagonally across from it. This is the best way for it to show if the desired temperature is really being maintained.

Rainbowfish can also be kept in a beautifully planted tank. Even species from waters without vegetation are very happy there. However, some species like to nibble at these plants. You can prevent this by offering the fish enough other vegetarian food.

Aquatic plants are useful also for purposes other than aesthetic:

✔ They can help break down nitrate in the water.

✔ They increase the oxygen level during the day.

✔ They provide cover in conflicts or when the females are harassed too much.

✔ They can serve as a spawning substrate and can offer growing fry places to hide.

Photo right: Indian Marshweed (**Limnophylla [Limnophila] indica**) *from northern and eastern Australia. Photo left: The decorative starplant* (**Eusteralis stellata**) *comes from northern Australia and southern Asia.*

Water hyssop *(Bacopa sp.)*: Found in Australia, Africa, Asia, and America. Undemanding in the aquarium. Sandy substrate and average light intensity are sufficient. Pruning encourages bushy appearance.

Ottelia *(Ottelia alismoides)*: Found in tropical Australia, on the eastern coast of Australia, and in New Guinea and southeastern Asia. Requires lots of light and good soil. Only suitable for larger tanks. Is very brittle.

Starplant *(Eusteralis stellata)*: Distributed throughout tropical Australia and eastern and southeastern Asia. Needs lots of light. Grows better in fine sand. Must be treated regularly with iron fertilizer.

Indian Marshweed *(Limnophylla [Limnophila] indica)*: Native to northeastern Australia as well as Africa and Asia. Fast-growing bunch plant that presents no problems. Bright light and regular fertilization required.

Elongated Swordplant *(Aponogeton elongatus)*: Grows in northeastern and tropical Australia. Requires little light. Splendid tuberous-rooted plant, which needs a resting period occasionally.

Willow-leaf Hygrophila *(Hygrophylla [Hygrophila] salicifolia)*: Distributed throughout tropical Australia and southeastern Asia. Only seen to best advantage in large aquaria. Likes lots of light. Otherwise few requirements. Rainbowfish like to nibble at it if they do not get enough other vegetarian food.

Eel grass *(Vallisneria sp.)*: Distributed worldwide. Well suited for aquaria; even grows in poor light. Propagation by runners.

Plants for Rainbowfish

Several species of aquatic plants are well suited for cultivation in the rainbowfish aquarium. Among these are:

✔ water trumpet (*Cryptocoryne*)
✔ water aspidistra (*Anubias*)
✔ Amazon swordplant (*Echinodorus*)
✔ arrowhead (*Sagittaria*)
✔ waterweed (*Egeria, Lagarosiphon*)
✔ fanwort (*Cabomba*)
✔ bottom nettle (*Hydrilla*)
✔ water milfoil (*Myriophyllum*)

Checklist
What Plants Require

1 Nutrients: They get fertilizer as bacteria break down fish waste products into nitrate. Commercially available fertilizers can also be applied.

2 Carbon dioxide (CO_2): This gas is breathed out by the fish. It can also be given supplementally using equipment available from specialty stores.

3 Light: A lighting duration of 12–14 hours per day is important. With the help of light, plants absorb CO_2 from the water and release oxygen back into the water.

4 Substrate: Coarse, unwashed, calcium-free sand with a covering of washed gravel in a variety of sizes.

5 Regular water changes: These are appreciated by fish and plants.

HOW-TO: FEEDING

Dried Foods

This food is certainly the most convenient for aquarists. It is offered as flakes, extruded pellets, tablets, sticks, or granules. Vitamins and trace elements important for the health of the fish are usually added. Because both of these additives are perishable, dried foods with these additives should only be bought in small quantities and at pet stores with a large turnover.

Dried food consists primarily of either animal or vegetable matter. Dyes like carotene are added to many types. This is advantageous for red-colored fish species because their colors are enhanced.

It is not bad if the food sinks to the bottom. Many rainbowfish look for food there, too. This behavior can also be observed in the wild. They nibble at boulders or similar objects to eat the algae or animals which live in it. For this reason, many species have fleshy lips with many tiny external teeth.

Live Foods

Live food is a welcome change for fish. You can catch live food in clean ponds or streams, buy it in the pet store, or, if you have the space and the patience, even raise it yourself.

Good live foods include:

✔ Water fleas (*Daphnia*)
✔ Copepods (*Cyclops* and *Diaptomus*)
✔ Cladocerans (*Bosmina*)
✔ Bloodworms (*Chirinomos*): Do not feed too often because they can cause severe allergies in many people upon contact.
✔ Phantom larvae, glassworms (*Corethra*)
✔ Mosquito larvae (*Culex*): Before feeding, freeze them so that you are not plagued later by mosquitoes in your house.
✔ Sludgeworms (*Tubifex*): Although, highly nutritious, they must be rinsed in water for at least 1 week before feeding. Either change the water frequently or put the container with the worms under a dripping faucet. Always keep tubifex refrigerated.

Frozen Food

Frozen food is a good substitute for live food. Pet stores offer frozen mosquito larvae, prawns, mussels, or squid. Frozen food should be thawed with

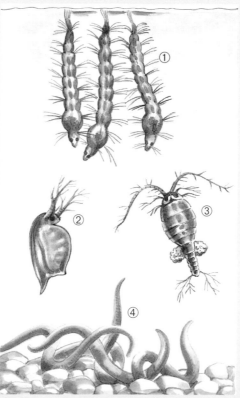

Live foods: ① black mosquito larvae, ② water fleas, ③ copepods, ④ tubifex.

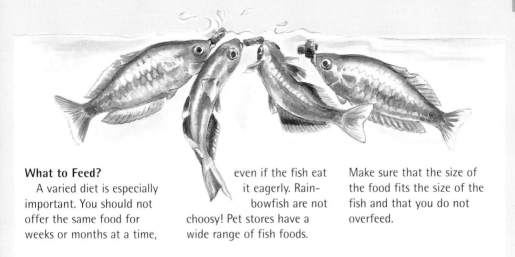

What to Feed?

A varied diet is especially important. You should not offer the same food for weeks or months at a time, even if the fish eat it eagerly. Rainbowfish are not choosy! Pet stores have a wide range of fish foods. Make sure that the size of the food fits the size of the fish and that you do not overfeed.

lukewarm water and washed in a fine sieve. If necessary, cut up the frozen food before feeding it to your fish.

Important: Store frozen food in the freezer compartment of the refrigerator so that it does not spoil.

Collecting Live Food Yourself

✔ In water: Be careful that no parasites, such as fish lice or flukes, or other unwelcome guests, like freshwater polyps (*Hydra*) and flatworms (*Planaria*), are brought in to the aquarium in the process. That is why it is better to put freshly caught food in a clean container initially and then take it out carefully later.

✔ Meadow insects, such as small grasshoppers, are good food and are always eagerly accepted. Make sure, however, that the meadows where you trap the insects have not been sprayed with toxic chemicals. First, refrigerate the insects to kill them, and then cut them up into bite-size pieces for feeding.

Dried food also comes in the form of large tablets.

Biotope Aquaria

Well-chosen plants can help you simulate a specific biotope.

✔ Dimly lit forest stream aquarium with swordplants (*Aponogeton*), water trumpets (*Cryptocoryne*), or water aspidistras (*Anubias*). In a tank like this, many fish species from the *Melanotaenia-goldiei* group are seen to best advantage.

✔ Brightly lit aquarium: Amazon swordplants (*Echinodorus*), swordplants (*Aponogeton*), ottelia (*Ottelia*), or fine-leafed starplant (*Eusteralis*). Such tanks are suitable for Splendid or Threadfin Rainbowfish.

Important: Leave enough swimming space for your fish.

What They Eat

Rainbowfish eat both animal and vegetable food. In the wild, they eat whatever is available, as long as they can swallow it.

Studies of the stomach contents of rainbowfish living in the wild have shown that about 40 percent of their diet consisted of terrestrial insects such as ants. Tiny aquatic crustaceans like water fleas (*Daphnia* and others) represented another 37 percent

of their diet. Aquatic insects and insect larvae, such as mosquito larvae, accounted for 18 percent. Algae and plant seeds made up the remainder.

Naturally, such a list can change drastically, because the range of foods depends mainly on the particular habitat of the fish species, the season of the year, and the weather. Many species can even go without food for prolonged periods without much harm.

How Often Should You Feed Your Fish?

You can easily be tempted to overfeed your rainbowfish. This is because of the behavior of the fish. As soon as they see their caretaker, they swim excitedly back and forth at the front of the aquarium. When they receive some food, they behave almost like piranhas. Do not be influenced by this begging!

✔ Feed a varied diet.

✔ Feed only in small amounts.

✔ It would be ideal to feed three to five times a day in tiny portions, because that would most mimic the way they feed in nature. Even feeding once a day is perfectly all right, as long as you give a bit more.

Two displaying male Red Rainbowfish (G. incisus). 5.5 in. (14 cm).

✔ Only feed as much as the fish can eat in 5 minutes.

✔ 1–2 days without food per week does no harm.

If you do not stick to these rules, don't be surprised if your fish get fat, no longer look good, and are incapable of reproduction.

Preventing Disease

Rainbowfish are very resistant animals which often survive in natural aquatic environments with unbelievably poor water conditions. For this reason, they also rarely get sick in the aquarium.

Pathogens, such as parasites, bacteria, or viruses, live in all aquaria and naturally belong to the habitat of the fish in the wild as well. They only cause problems when living conditions deteriorate and when the fish are in a weakened condition. These conditions will allow the pathogens to multiply excessively.

You can prevent this by:

✔ Always ensuring good water quality.

✔ Using biological filters.

✔ Carrying out partial water changes regularly.

✔ Forcing yourself to limit the size of your fish population.

These measures have kept my rainbowfish free of diseases such as white spot, dropsy, or fin and tail rot, which attack other fish from time to time.

Velvet Disease

Years ago, velvet disease was a plague, and rainbowfish responded poorly to treatment. I keep the disease in check with a very old method that is almost forgotten today: In each of my tanks there is a copper scouring pad, like the ones used for cleaning cooking pots (available in any supermarket). It is replaced once a year.

CARE DURING VACATION

Few other aquarium fish require less care during vacation than rainbowfish. I leave my fish on their own for up to 4 weeks. This duration is only possible because none of my many tanks is overstocked and because the water quality barely deteriorates even without regular water changes.

✔ *2 days before departure and immediately after returning home, I change one third of the water.*

✔ *A timer regulates lighting and heating.*

✔ *A fellow aquarist checks my fish once a week.*

✔ *No feeding! Even in nature, rainbowfish must often manage for a long time without food.*

If you cannot be so "radical" then ask a fellow aquarist to look after your fish. But make it clear that under no circumstances should your fish be overfed.

You can also use an automatic food dispenser. You should test this device thoroughly before using it.

Fish Tuberculosis

This is the most common of all bacterial diseases, but don't worry—it's not infectious to people. Almost 80 percent of all aquarium fish carry latent tuberculosis infections, and fish tuberculosis can easily be transferred from new fish because it is difficult to recognize infected fish at the time of purchase. Even in the aquarium, the disease often can remain undetected for a long time.

The disease can attack all fish, especially in heavily overstocked tanks with poor water quality. In recent years, it has also become a problem with rainbowfish (see table, page 47).

Unfortunately, no effective medication is available to treat it, and the fish should be euthanized as quickly and painlessly as possible.

Important Note: Again, fish tuberculosis can be very contagious between fish in your tank. However, not all rainbowfish seem to be affected by it.

If the above-mentioned symptoms occur repeatedly in the aquarium, the only remedy is to destroy the entire stock. Then, empty the aquarium, and disinfect it with a chlorine solution. You can then set it up again from scratch.

All diseases can be avoided with proper care, regular water changes, and a moderately stocked aquarium. If diseases do appear at some time, do not resort to medications right away. First, try to determine the real reasons for the outbreak and eliminate them. Medications should only support your efforts.

Important Note: Most fish medications are colored liquids, or tablets that look similar to candy. Keep them out of the reach of children.

Flatulence

When rainbowfish devour large morsels of dried food too greedily, they can occasionally develop flatulence. This is recognized by the fact that the fish try desperately to swim to the bottom—without success. The buoyancy caused by the gases is often so great that the backs of the fish rise up out of the water, and they have problems with equilibrium. The gas usually escapes within a short time.

When rainbowfish eat dried food too greedily, they can develop flatulence.

Fish Diseases and Their Treatment

Diseases	Symptoms	Treatment
White spot, ich (*Ichthyophthirius multifiliis*)	Fish are covered with white spots and nodules; do not eat; twitch their fins.	Several medications are available from specialty stores. Use according to directions, and then change the water.
Velvet disease (*Oodinium pillularis*)	A dense coating of tiny yellowish spots give the scales a velvety appearance. Often affects only the gills. The fish usually have difficulty breathing and often hang at the water surface.	Ask the pet dealer for advice. Be careful when using medications, because the dose required can be lethal for rainbowfish as well.
Columnaris disease (*Flexibaxter [Flexibacter] columnaris*)	White coating on the lips and edges of the fins. Usually occurs only with poor water quality.	Several partial water changes over several days. Medication according to directions.
Dropsy	Swollen body with scales sticking out; protruding eyes.	Various medications are available from the pet store. Use according to directions, and then change the water.
Fin and tail rot	Fins are ragged, often shortened; borders of the fins can be white.	Several medications are available from the pet store. Use according to directions, and then change the water.
Fish tuberculosis (*Mycobacterium sp.*)	Swollen body with scales sticking out or emaciated appearance with loss of color. Small wounds that do not heal on the body, tumor-like growths on the fins, gills, mouth, or eyes.	No known effective treatment; euthanize the fish as quickly and painlessly as possible.
pH of the water too high/low	Fish dart around in the tank; jump.	Test pH immediately and change water.
Nitrate poisoning	Fish swim at the water surface breathing heavily and appear in breeding colors.	Carry out partial water changes immediately, repeat a few hours later if necessary.

Once a tank has been broken in and your fish have become used to their new home, you can sit in front of the aquarium at your leisure and observe the lively goings-on of your fish in the tank. In the process, you will certainly be able to recognize many types of behavior.

The Aquarium As Study Object

One often hears or reads that fish in an aquarium are boring and that they only swim from one side to the other and back again. These people have certainly never sat in front of a properly equipped tank and watched the activity behind the glass. On closer observation, one can recognize various types of fish behavior, such as display or courtship.

Colors play an important role in this respect. Rainbowfish are appropriately named, because under the right lighting they shimmer in all the colors of the rainbow. Many species can vary the color of their body in a flash. The Lake Kutubu Rainbowfish, for instance, changes its coloring from pure black to black and silver, blue and silver, turquoise and gold, and finally pure gold.

Life in the School

Wild rainbowfish are gregarious creatures that frequently spend their time in schools at the water surface and keep watch together for insects that have fallen into the water.

Life in the school has two advantages for the fish:

✔ When there are many fish, a potential enemy has a hard time concentrating on a single animal.

✔ The probability of being eaten drops for the individual fish as the size of the school in which it lives increases.

You can also observe this schooling behavior in the aquarium. The fish come together quickly in a group when they sense danger or when they have just been put into a tank.

For this reason, rainbowfish should always be kept in schools. As you already know, these beautiful fish can also be kept in community tanks with other fish species, as long as the requirements of all fish are similar.

You can get a good impression of their behavior, however, with a species tank. This does not mean that there can only be a small school of a single species of rainbowfish in this aquarium, but rather that you can keep two to four species together in the same tank.

Two courting male Crimson-spotted Rainbowfish [Large Rainbowfish] (**M. douboulayi**) *from the Noosa River. 3.1 in. (8 cm).*

TIP

Observe Closely

Until recently, rainbowfish, despite their beauty, were somewhat neglected in the field of aquariology; they were not kept in aquariums as frequently as guppies, neon tetras, or cichlids. But all that has changed. Through the exploration of areas where no one had ever looked for rainbowfish, many species have recently been discovered. As a result, the number of known species has nearly doubled within the last 15 years. For this reason, many species are still "new territory" for aquarists. So, observe your fish closely—perhaps you will succeed in discovering as yet unknown information about their care, behavior, or breeding.

I suggest that you keep a fish diary to jot down your observations along with time of day and external conditions, for example before or after feeding, changing the water, or turning on the light. If you notice things for which you can find no explanation in the literature, do not be afraid to pass these observations along to members of aquarium societies or the International Rainbowfish Association. For addresses, see page 62.

If you want to breed your fish, you should make sure that the species are not too closely related, because the females are sometimes difficult to tell apart. In nature, up to four species are found together in the same body of water, often swimming in mixed groups as well. Usually, though, there are only two species, and these are always easy to tell apart, even their females. Lakes are often inhabited by only one species.

Males Are Quarrelsome

In my experience, it pays to keep more males than females together—no matter which species. Males of all species are relatively aggressive toward others of their kind and often toward males of other species as well. This can sometimes lead to injuries or even to death.

If you keep several males together, the disputes normally run their course without problems. Quite the contrary: Dominant males always try to show themselves in their best colors. Because this is seldom tolerated by the other males, they usually all appear in their full colors. The males are occupied with each other in this way most of the day. As a result, the aquarist always sees fish in full coloration.

When Something Is Wrong

In the course of your daily inspections, if you have noticed that the fish do not display this typical behavior at least in the morning hours, it is usually time to take a closer look at the aquarium.

Test the water quality in the tank, and—if necessary—change the water. The fish should then resume their "courtship game."

Naturally, there are also other reasons why the males are not interested in putting on their "show."

✔ The water is too cold or too warm.
✔ The fish are sick.

You should also carry out a partial water change immediately if the fish:

✔ are hanging at the water surface breathing heavily,
✔ dash about aimlessly in the tank.

Test the pH afterwards, and slowly neutralize the water should it still be necessary.

Exceptions to the Rule

Showing full coloration and "playful" behavior are not always a sign of well being. In Ornate Rainbowfish (*Rhadinocentrus ornatus*), it can also mean that the fish are suffering from nitrate poisoning. Before long, they display obvious difficulty breathing, and soon after that, often still splendidly colored, they hang below the water surface and die within a few minutes if you do not change the water. This species reacts very suddenly to a deterioration of water quality in the aquarium. Regular water changes and monitoring water conditions are especially important for their care.

The Ornate and also the Cairns Rainbowfish (*Cairnsichthys rhombosomoides*) are considered the delicate representatives of this robust fish family. Often, they do not survive capture from the wild. No cause has been found for this unfortunate reaction. This is not always the case, however, and animals that survive capture and transport quickly get used to being kept in the aquarium and reproduce without hesitation.

An unusually severe fright can also lead to death. A small school of Cairns Rainbowfish that I had kept for 2 years died suddenly in my tank as I was doing some welding on an aquarium stand. In contrast to this, the flashing light from the welding equipment stimulated other rainbowfish at the same time to begin courtship and spawning. In nature, too, one can observe rainbowfish courting when a storm with thunder and lightning occurs.

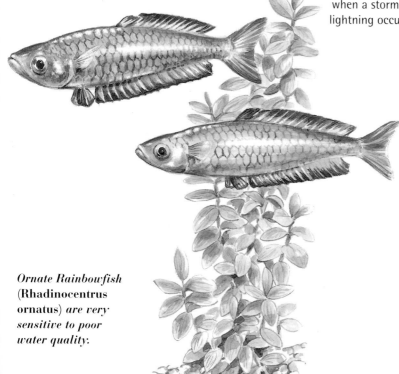

*Ornate Rainbowfish
(**Rhadinocentrus
ornatus**) are very
sensitive to poor
water quality.*

BEHAVIOR
INTERPRETER

This is how rainbowfish communicate among themselves, but also with you.

 The rainbowfish displays this behavior.

 What does the rainbowfish mean by it?

 This is how I respond correctly to its behavior!

 A male Red Rainbowfish is performing a courtship display before a female.

 The male wants to impress the female.

 Observe carefully, do not disturb.

The male Red Rainbowfish does a headstand in front of the female.

The male wants to induce the female to spawn.

Observe carefully, do not disturb.

 The pair of Red Rainbowfish separates rapidly, beating their tails.

 They have just spawned and are now swirling the eggs and sperm.

 You can look forward to offspring.

 The pair of Red Rainbowfish swims trembling side by side.

 The fish are spawning.

 Observe carefully, do not disturb.

🐟 A male Eastern Rainbowfish [Eastern Splendid Rainbowfish] swims around a female.

❓ He is trying to induce her to mate.

❗ Observe, but do not disturb.

Ornate Rainbowfish 👉 males display full colors and race around the tank.

They are displaying. ❓

If you have only ❗ two males in the tank, the subordinate one can be chased to death. Therefore, keep several males.

👆 A young fish carries an egg in its mouth.

❓ He is feeding on the eggs and larvae of his siblings.

❗ To keep the fry from eating the spawn, you should put the eggs in a separate tank.

Bleher's Rainbowfish males intermittently 👉 flash colorful stripes from the snout to the first dorsal fin.

The males are displaying. ❓

Enjoy the show, but do not disturb. ❗

🐟 A male Arfak Rainbowfish holds his fins in the normal position.

❓ He has no reason to display because no other member of his species is present.

❗ Observe the fish. If this behavior continues, the fish may be sick.

TIP

Observing Spawning Behavior

Rainbowfish prefer to spawn in the early morning hours. If you want to observe the spawning behavior but are not an early riser, here is a trick: Set the timer in your aquarium so that the lights go on when you have the time to watch.

This trick will only work, however, if the aquarium is located in a dark place during the day.

Reproduction

Rainbowfish are continuous spawners. This means that in the wild they spawn throughout the year as long as the water quality in their habitats allows it. If concentrations of organic substances and minerals become too high because of constant evaporation of the water, the fish stop spawning.

If the water level then suddenly rises again after a downpour and the entire stream, river, or lake awakes to new life, then it is usually not long until the fish, too, begin thinking of reproduction.

With the fresh water and the extensive flooding often caused by it, new nutrients enter the ponds and streams, revitalizing the food chain. Algae and tiny creatures (plankton) suddenly begin reproducing and provide a plentiful food supply for the hatching larvae and countless fry which appear 1–3 weeks after the start of the rain.

Because rainbowfish spawn continuously from this point on, freshly deposited eggs, hatching larvae, and younger fry form a part of the diet of their older brothers and sisters. In my experience, however, adult rainbowfish very seldom cannabilize their offspring.

Breeding at Home

In the home aquarium, as in the wild, you can observe how after a water change, the rainbowfish immediately begin courtship and spawning.

Tip: I have learned that rainbowfish and blue-eyes can be stimulated to courtship and subsequent spawning by the light from photographic flash units. Since then, I have taken advantage of this fact when photographing fish.

Breeding rainbowfish is not difficult and is even possible for novice aquarists. Rearing the fry of most species also presents few problems. However, a few basic requirements and conditions must be met:

✔ It is best to keep three males and two females in your tank (to differentiate between the sexes, see page 55).

✔ Because many young fish are cannibals, you should offer the larvae and fry hiding places, such as roots or floating plants (Indian Fern).

✔ If you want to breed your fish, you should only keep species that are not too similar in the same tank. In so doing, you prevent hybridization. This is necessary for protection of the species.

Requirements for Breeding

Although rainbowfish are continuous spawners in aquariological terminology, this is true only to a limited extent. They seldom spawn all day long, but rather in the early morning hours, as a rule.

Not all females spawn on successive days. Much depends on their physical condition and their readiness to spawn. You must take this into consideration when breeding your fish in an aquarium.

Males in good condition are always ready to mate, as long as the water quality is to their liking. The ideal breeding group consists of at least three males of approximately the same size and two females. The fish begin with courtship and spawning soon after being put into the breeding tank.

Depending on the condition of the females, they can be left in the tank for several days. If they show signs of fatigue, it is best to remove all animals from the breeding tank, and keep the sexes apart and well fed for a while.

If you remove the eggs from the breeding tank, separate the sexes with a tank divider made of glass or some other material until the females are again ready to spawn.

Differentiating between the Sexes

Many rainbowfish species change their body shape con- siderably with increasing age. This is especially true for males, which can become very deep-bodied, depending on the species.

✔ The males also differ from the females in having more intense colors and elongated fin rays of the first dorsal fin. The second dorsal fin and the anal fin are enlarged in many species, and both are pointed posteriorly.

✔ In the females, the posterior edge of the second dorsal fin and the anal fin is rounded.

In many species, differences between the sexes in coloration and finnage are extreme.

Main Occupation: Courtship

The most interesting and exciting part in the reproductive behavior of rainbowfish is the courtship display. Both sexes appear in their most beautiful colors. The males, however, are far more intensely colored.

The males of most species display a bright stripe that can be turned on and off like a neon sign. This so-called "courtship stripe" extends from the upper lip to the anterior rays of the first dorsal fin and can, depending on the species, be snow white, yellow, orange, rusty brown, or bright blue. The females of many species also display these stripes during courtship, although much less intense.

Rainbowfish that do not display this courtship stripe include all forms of the Splendid Rainbowfish, all known forms allied with the Lake Eacham

Doing a headstand, a male rainbowfish shows a female the spawning site.

Rainbowfish, as well as the species Parkinson's, Crimson-spotted [Large], and Murray River [Inland] Rainbowfish. The males of some representatives of these forms are capable of a slight change in the color of the uppermost row of scales on each side of the body, which extends along the entire length of the body. However, no courtship stripe is percent.

Indicating the Spawning Site

The males of species that display the courtship stripe swim rapidly around their partners with fully extended fins. They often perform proper "headstands," during which the pulsating stripe is always turned toward the female. This behavior is a way to entice

A pair of Red Rainbowfish (Glossolepis incisus) approaches the spawning site in a tangle of plant stems.

the female gradually to the selected spawning site.

Except for the headstand, the courtship behavior of males without courtship stripes is the same.

The Spawning Site

In the wild, the spawning site can be located in a tangle of plants among the feathery stream-washed roots of trees growing along the bank, mats of algae, or similar locations.

All species that display the courtship stripe (see page 56) always spawn—as far as is known—in dark, hidden places. Rainbowfish that do not display the courtship stripe seem, on the other hand, to prefer open sunny spawning sites near the surface.

In the aquarium, aquatic plants with finely divided leaves or artificial spawning substrates are usually accepted.

Spawning

A female who is ready to spawn will follow the male to the particular spawning site. The fish swim close together side by side. You can tell the eggs and sperm have been released by the fact that the fishes' bodies and fins vibrate for a few seconds. Afterwards, the fish dart apart with lightning speed, whirling up the expelled eggs and sperm in the process. Depending on the species and physical condition of the females, 2–3 or even 200, or more rarely still, 300 eggs are laid in this manner.

The eggs are equipped with long, very thin threads which attach to the spawning substrate. The threads contract spirally and thus pull the eggs in close to the substrate. The round eggs, 1–2 mm in diameter, can appear clear or slightly milky, depending on the species.

Checklist
Breeding Correctly

1 For the best breeding results, you need at least three males of approximately the same size and two females.

2 Breeding and rearing tanks should be at least 3 feet (1 m) long.

3 The breeding tank should be filled with fresh, aged water that has the same temperature or is 4 to 6°F warmer than that in the display tank.

4 The water hardness should be somewhat lower and the pH value the same as in the display tank.

5 An internal filtration system is desirable, but not necessary. Without a filter you must aerate.

6 Use fine-leaved plants, fine roots, or "spawning mops" (see page 58) made of brown acrylic yarn as a spawning substrate.

7 Examine the plants or mops daily for eggs.

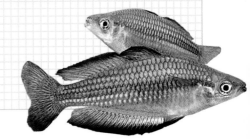

Artificial Spawning Substrate

"Mops" made of brown acrylic yarn and attached to a float (cork) have proved especially successful as a spawning substrate. They can easily be removed from the breeding tank, checked daily for eggs, and, if desired, transferred to a separate rearing tank. The strands should reach to the bottom, because many rainbowfish prefer to spawn on the tank bottom.

Development of the Young

The larvae hatch from the eggs after 4–14 days, depending on the species and the water temperature. They have a greatly reduced yolk sack, fill their swim bladders within 12 hours, and can then be observed as tiny "streaks" swimming directly under the surface.

With good feeding the fry grow very quickly in the first weeks, and small species are fully grown in a few months. Large species, however, need 2–3 years to reach maturity. Most species are already capable of reproduction when they have reached one third of their final body size.

Rearing the Fry

Rainbowfish will reproduce even without much assistance from the keeper, and a few fry always manage to reach maturity. If you specifically want offspring, then you must provide certain conditions.

✔ The fish should be placed in a breeding tank. The tank should not be too small, even for small species, because courtship and mating can take up a lot of room and the fish need space to swim. I have had the best experience with breeding tanks at least 3.4 ft. (1 m) in length.

✔ Fresh, aged water, whose temperature does not necessarily have to be higher than that in the tank where the breeding animals live.

✔ A little gravel is a good substrate; better yet is a layer of shell grit.

✔ A small internal filter is usually adequate.

✔ Fine-leaved aquatic plants such as Java Moss, ambulina, or water milfoil can be used as a spawning substrate. Other plants, fine roots, or similar objects are also accepted.

✔ Hiding places such as roots where the fish larvae can find cover.

Feeding the Fry

As soon as the fish larvae are visible at the water surface, they should be fed a little food that drifts on the surface. Commercial powdered fry food or even very finely ground flake food are excellent. You can also use liquid food specially developed for fry or small live foods to supplement their diet.

Some suitable first foods are:

✔ Infusoria, tiny single-celled creatures, which you have prepared in advance. To culture them, take pieces of turnip the size of a sugar cube, dry them in the oven, and pulverize them. Put the powdered turnip in a glass of water. Place this, uncovered, in a shady spot. The infusoria will have developed after about 1 week. Feed them with banana peels.

✔ Nauplii, the larvae of brine shrimp: You can buy the dried eggs in the pet store. Put the eggs in saltwater (about 1 oz. [20 g] sea salt to .24 cups [1 L] water), and allow the glass to stand at about 78°F (25°C). Aeration is necessary. The nauplii hatch after 1–2 days.

✔ Vinegar eels, about ⅛-in. (2-mm) long nematodes which live in fermenting liquids.

Important: Never feed your fry copepods (*Cyclops*). They are predatory and will attack the larvae and fish in the breeding tank.

Adjust the size of the food to the growth of the fish. With increasing size, the food should become more varied.

How Often to Feed?

It is best to feed larvae and fry more frequently, but in smaller amounts. Although ideal, this solution is usually impossible to carry out in practice.

Therefore, I recommend feeding once in the morning and once in the evening.

Care of the Spawn

Take the spawning substrate out of the water, squeeze out some of the water, and examine the individual strands. The eggs are easy to recognize, because they often stick together in groups of two or more. Protect the eggs from egg predation by putting the spawning substrate in a separate tank.

It is important to check the water quality in the rearing tank constantly and change the water often. You must proceed carefully when doing this. If you are serious about breeding, then you need several rearing tanks to be able to sort the offspring according to size. Fry of all rainbowfish species are cannibals (see page 53): they eat the spawn and hunt small fish.

Displaying male
Banded Rainbowfish
(Melanotaenia
trifasciata). Body
length 3.9 in.
(10 cm).

Addresses

Rainbowfish Study Group of
    North America
Attn: Sherry Taylor
171 Campbell Lane
Cookville, TN 38501

Rainbowfish Study Group
Attn: Gary Lange
2590 Cheshire
Floissant, MO 63033
www.netpets.com

Home of the Rainbowfish
www.ecn.net.au
e-mail: atappin@ecn.net.au

Native Fish Australia
P.O. Box 162
Doncaster Victoria 3108
Australia
www.nativefish.asn.au

International Rainbowfish
    Association
Secretary: Andreas Deutrich
Rather Street 53
D-52353 Düren [Germany]

Useful Books

Allen, Gerald. *Rainbowfishes: In
    Nature and in the Aquarium.*
    Tetra Verlag, Melle, Germany.
    1995.
Carrington, N: *A Fishkeeper's
    Guide to a Healthy Aquarium.*
    Tetra Press, Morris Plains, NJ.
    1990.
Schliewen, Ulrich: *Aquarium Fish.*
    Barron's Educational Series, Inc.,
    Hauppauge, New York. 1992.
Stadelmann, P. *The Natural
    Aquarium Handbook.* Barron's
    Educational Series, Inc.,
    Hauppauge, New York. 2000.

Periodicals

The Rainbow Times, Rainbowfish
    Study Group, Cookville, TN.
Tropical Fish Hobbyist, T.F.H. Pub-
    lications, Inc., Neptune City, NJ.
Aquarium Fish magazine, Fancy
    Publications, Boulder, CO.

The Author and Photographer

Gunther Schmida has been a passionate vivarium hobbyist and photographer for over 40 years. His special interests involve the fish, frog, and reptile fauna of Australia and New Guinea. Rainbowfish are of special concern to him. He is the co-author of the first complete book on Australian freshwater fish as well as the author/photographer of a comprehensive work on the above-mentioned fauna. His articles/photos appear in magazines worldwide, as well as in DATZ.

The Artist

Renate Holzner works as a freelance illustrator. Her broad repertoire extends from line drawings and photorealistic illustrations to computer graphics.

Acknowledgment

The author and publisher wish to thank the many friends and fellow aquarists, without whose unselfish help this guide would never have come about. In Australia, thanks are due especially to Terry Adams, Dr. Gerald Allen, Neil Armstrong, Barry Beck, Ron Bowman, Steve Brooks, Wayne Buglar, Rob Carroll, Adrian Dawson, Dr. Bruce Hanson, Gordon Hydes, Peter Krauss, Ray Legget, Gary Lenehan, Brian and Glenn McGregor, Keith Martin, Robert Pulvirenti, Dean Sampson, Ken Shaw, Heinz Staude, Adrian Tappin, Rob Wager, Dave Wilson and many other members of ANGFA (Australia New Guinea Fish Association). In Germany, thanks go to Dr. Jürgen Clasen and Norbert Grunwald of the International Rainbowfish Association as well as Heiko Bleher in Italy.

Photos: Cover and Inside

Front cover: Two displaying male Checkered Rainbowfish [Checkered Splendid Rainbowfish] *(Melanotaenia s. inornata)*, 10 cm (large photo). Banded Rainbowfish *(Melanotaenia trifasciata)* from the Goyder River (small photo).

Back cover: Two male Boeseman's Rainbowfish *(Melanotaenia boesemani)*. 10 cm.

Page 1: Displaying male Sepik Rainbowfish *(Glossolepis multisquamatus)*. 9 cm.

Page 2–3: Male Bulolo Rainbowfish *(Chilatherina bulolo)* from the Erap River. 7 cm.

Page 4–5: Two male Crimson-spotted Rainbowfish [Large Rainbowfish] *(Melanotaenia duboulayi)* from Kangaroo Creek displaying. 8 cm.

Page 6–7: 10-cm-long male Eastern Rainbowfish [Eastern Splendid Rainbowfish] *(Melanotaenia s. splendida)*.

Page 64: Male Eastern Rainbowfish [Eastern Splendid Rainbowfish] *(Melanotaenia s. splendida)* from the Chlohesy River, northern Australia.

Important Information

Electrical devices for aquarium maintenance are described in this guide. It is imperative that you follow the advice on page 33 and the manufacturer's safety regulations, since serious accidents could result otherwise.

Before purchasing a large aquarium, have the load-bearing capacity of the floor at the intended location tested.

Water damage caused by breakage of the glass, overflowing, or leaking of the tank cannot always be avoided. Therefore, be sure to take out insurance (see page 11).

Fish medications and other preparations for treating the fish and the water must be kept away from children. Caustic chemicals should not be allowed to come in contact with eyes, mucous membranes, or skin. In case of contagious diseases (for example fish tuberculosis, see page 46), do not touch the infected fish with bare hands or reach into the tank.

English language edition published in 2000 by Barron's Educational Series, Inc.
Translated from the German by Mary Lynch.
©Copyright 1998 by Gräfe und Unzer Verlag GmbH, Munich, Germany

Original German title is *Regenbogenfische*

All inquiries should be addressed to:
Barron's Educational Series, Inc.
250 Wireless Boulevard
Hauppauge, NY 11788
http://www.barronseduc.com

Library of Congress Catalog Card No. 99-046856

International Standard Book No. 0-7641-1180-9

Library of Congress Cataloging-in-Publication Data
Schmida, Gunther E., 1942–
 [Regenbogenfische. English.]
 Rainbowfish / Gunther Schmida ; with photos by Gunther Schmida and illustrations by Renate Holzner.—English language ed.
  p. cm.
 Includes bibliographical references.
 ISBN 0-7641-1180-9
 1. Rainbowfish. 2. Aquariums. I. Title.
SF458.R35 S3613   2000
639.3'766—dc21   99-046856
                                  CIP

Printed in Hong Kong
9 8 7 6 5 4 3 2 1

1 Are rainbowfish suitable even for beginners?

No. Although most species are very robust, you should have some experience keeping fish.

2 Are rainbowfish recommended for community tanks?

They can easily be kept together with aquarium fish of similar size and temperament.

3 Are they aggressive towards other fish?

Males of all species can be very quarrelsome among themselves during courtship (see page 50).

4 Would it be better to keep them in a species tank or a special tank?

Not all. It depends on your interests. Small species and those considered to be delicate are seen to best advantage there.

5 Can species of different sizes be kept together?

It depends. In any case, it is best to group species of approximately the same size.

The expert answers the 10 most frequent questions about keeping rainbowfish.